TopReaders

Scary Sharks

Denise Ryan

Contents

There are about 400 kinds
of sharks in the world's oceans .
The most dangerous sharks
are bigger than people and
can swim much faster too!

What Is a Shark?

Sharks are fish. Some are small and flat. Others are large and round.

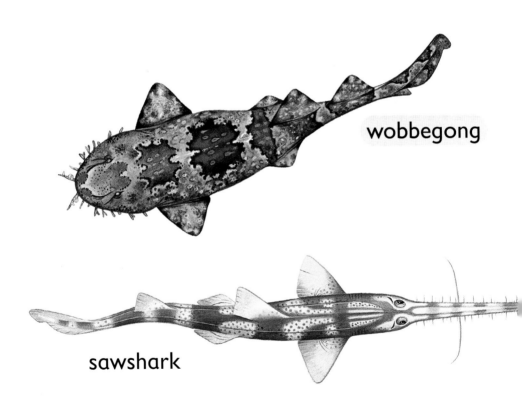

wobbegong

sawshark

All sharks have tails and fins.

lemon shark

oceanic whitetip

angelshark

Shark Sizes

Some sharks could fit into the palm of your hand. Others are as big as buses.

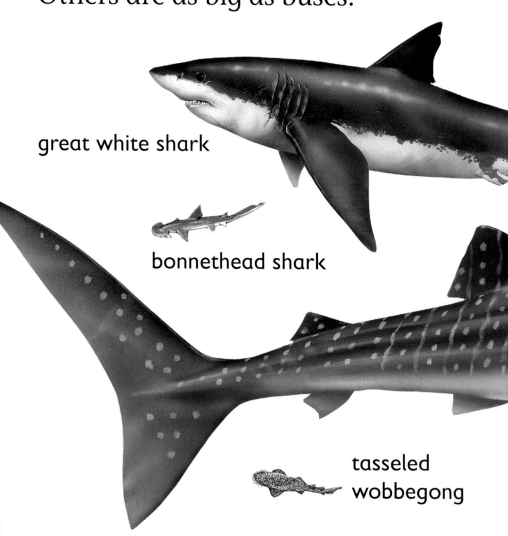

great white shark

bonnethead shark

tasseled wobbegong

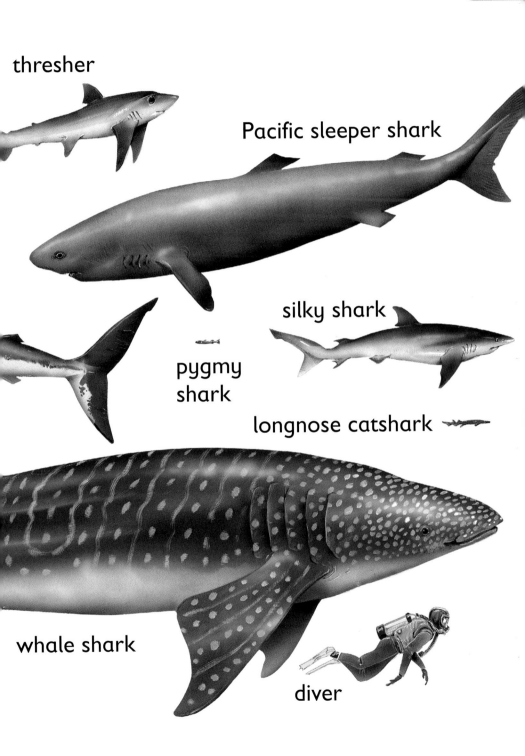

thresher

Pacific sleeper shark

silky shark

pygmy shark

longnose catshark

whale shark

diver

Ancient Sharks

The first sharks lived about 400 million years ago. We know about them because scientists have found and studied their fossil teeth.

Cladoselache was an ancient shark. It was a fast swimmer and could catch and swallow whole fish.

ancient shark

Cladoselache

Great Whites

Great whites are the scariest sharks. They are large, with sharp teeth and powerful jaws. They feed on seals, dolphins, and turtles.

great white shark

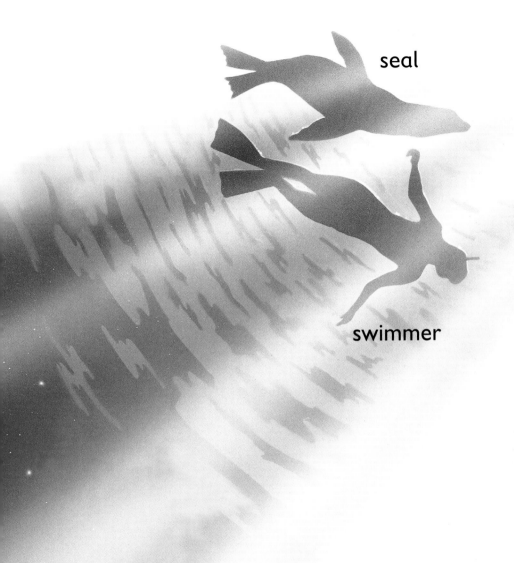

seal

swimmer

If a person swims in a great white's hunting area, the shark may think the swimmer is a seal and attack him or her.

Hammerheads

The strange-looking hammerhead shark has a wide, thick head with an eye at each end. Hammerheads live in groups in warm seas.

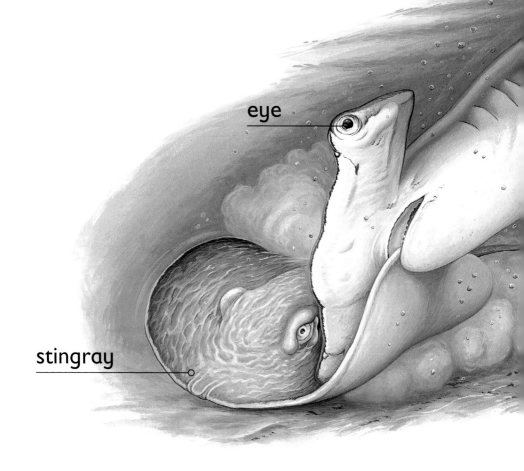

eye

stingray

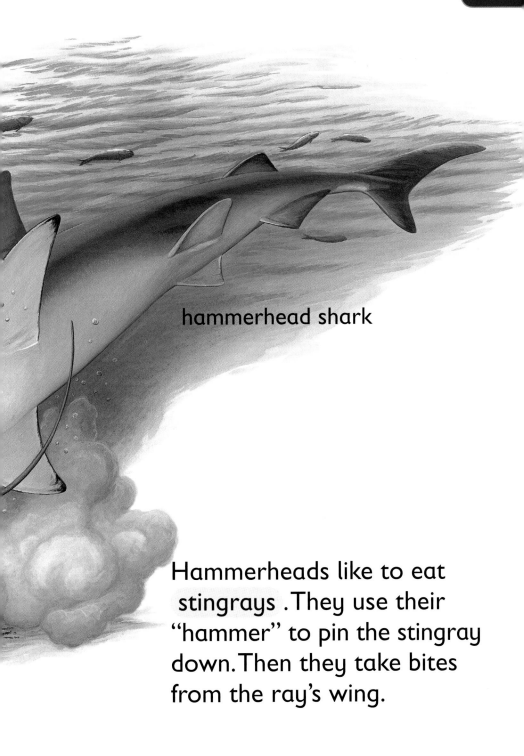

hammerhead shark

Hammerheads like to eat stingrays . They use their "hammer" to pin the stingray down. Then they take bites from the ray's wing.

Threshers

The tail of a thresher shark
is as long as the rest of its body.
Threshers use their long tails
to round up and kill fish.

thresher shark

Threshers have long side fins.
They help the shark to steer.

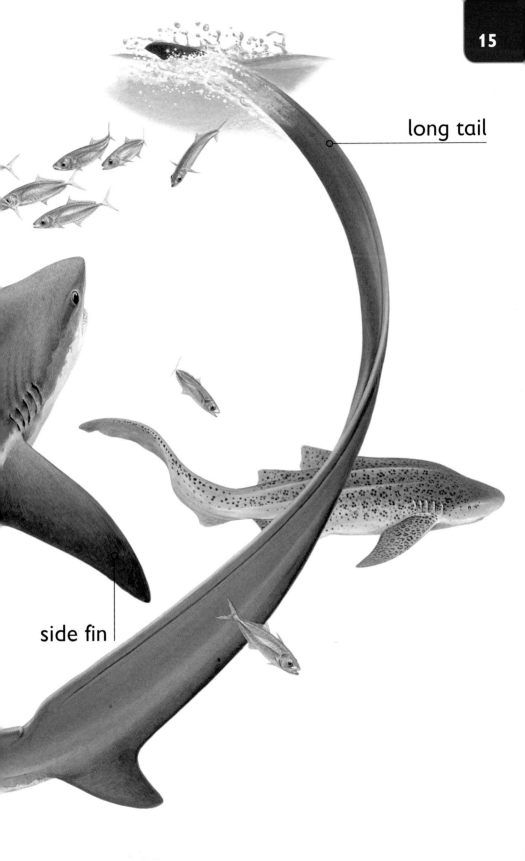

long tail

side fin

Whale Sharks

Whale sharks are the biggest sharks of all. They swim with their mouths open and suck up a "soup" of tiny plants and animals.

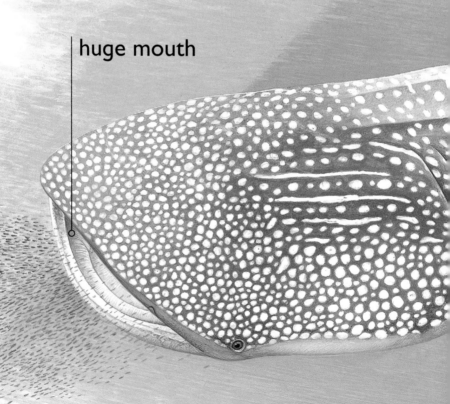

huge mouth

A whale shark is as big as
a school bus. Four people
could fit into its mouth.

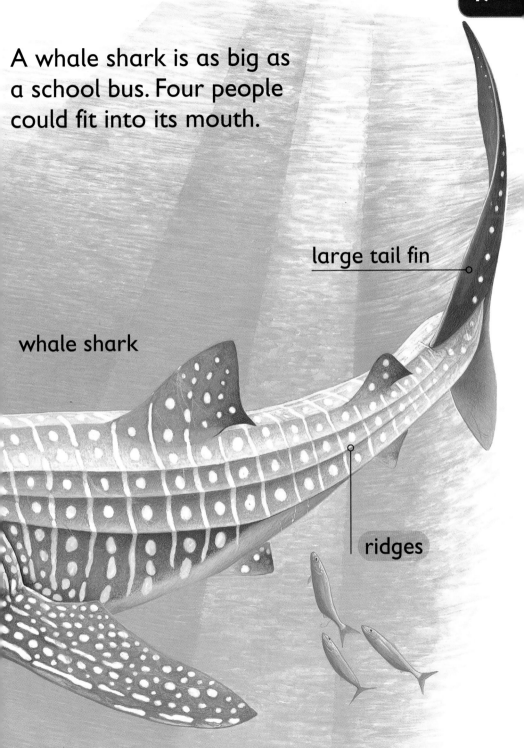

large tail fin

whale shark

ridges

Bull Sharks

Bull sharks swim in warm, shallow water near the coast. They will eat almost anything they can catch—including people!

bull shark

turtle

This bull shark
is hunting a turtle.

Spots and Stripes

Many sharks have spots and stripes on their skin. Some have whirls and patterns instead of spots and stripes.

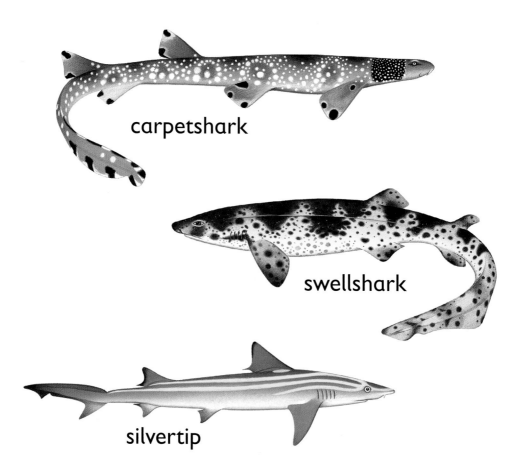

carpetshark

swellshark

silvertip

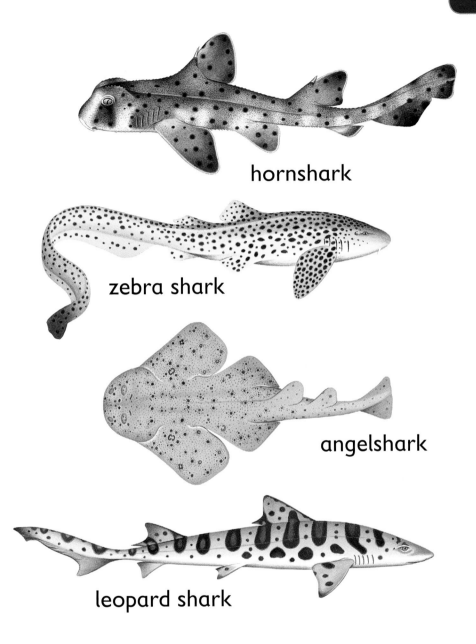

hornshark

zebra shark

angelshark

leopard shark

The marks on a shark's skin help it to hide safely among the rocks or on the seafloor.

Feeding

Tiny fish eat fish eggs. Small fish eat the tiny fish. Large fish eat the small fish. Then the shark eats the large fish!

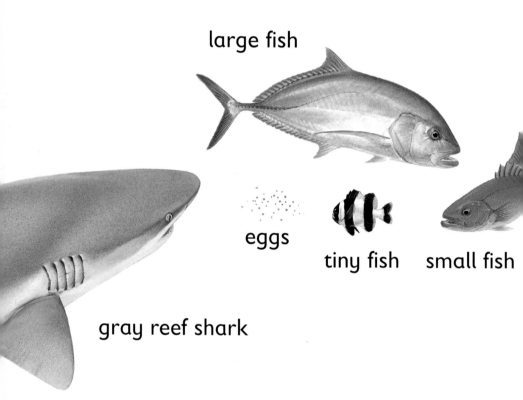

large fish

eggs

tiny fish   small fish

gray reef shark

The blacktip reef shark cruises coral reefs.

Watch Out!

Some sharks are like the trash cans of the sea. They will eat anything that comes their way.

tiger shark

This young seabird is learning to fly. Will it escape the jaws of the tiger shark?

seabird

Shark Friends

Pilot fish swim with sharks. They eat the scraps of food that the sharks miss. Remoras attach themselves to a shark so that they can ride with it.

remora

pilot fish

sandbar shark

Diving with Sharks

Trained divers dive into the sea to look closely at sharks. They need special equipment and dive in small groups so that they remain safe.

Divers keep their arms folded so they do not scare the sharks.

reef shark

Quiz

Can you match each shark with its name?

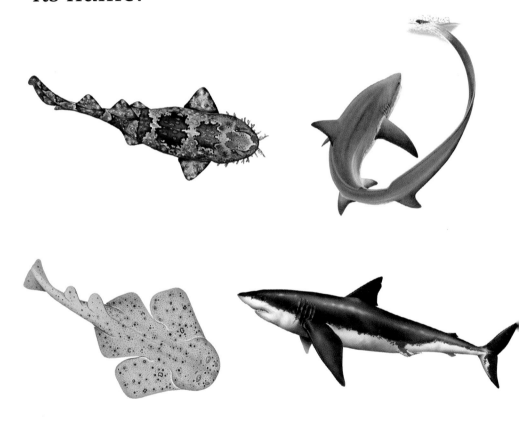

angelshark   wobbegong

great white   thresher

Glossary

ancient: very old

attack: to threaten or hurt someone

cruises: moves slowly

fossil: a hard part of an animal that died many years ago

oceans: Earth's very large areas of salt water

remoras: small fish that attach themselves to a shark

ridges: long, narrow, raised areas

scientists: people skilled or trained in science

stingrays: flat sea creatures related to sharks

whirls: swirly patterns

wobbegong: a kind of shark that lives on the seafloor

Index